O9-ABI-465

TABLE OF CONTENTS

If someone asked you to look at a rainbow, you would look up to the sky. Likewise, if someone asked you to think of something that shines, you would think of the sun. But not every rainbow or everything that shines can be found in the sky. Sometimes they are right under your feet.

Welcome to the world of gems, **minerals** that have been cut and polished to bring out the stone's color and fire. Fire describes the way gems seem to flash different colors of light, as if each stone contains a rainbow.

ROCK-HARD FACT

When you look into a gem, you're seeing more than shine and rainbow colors. You're looking into time itself. A gem is formed deep underground. Time, pressure, heat, and sometimes **erosion** very slowly change the rock. If conditions are just right, the product is a rough gemstone that took thousands of years—or more—to form.

THE BEAUTY BENEATH US

WHAT IS A MINERAL?

Minerals—made of **atoms** arranged in a **uniform** pattern—are the building blocks of rocks and gems.

FOR ROYALTY ONLY

Gems are so rare and valuable that they once belonged almost exclusively to royalty. Cleopatra of ancient Egypt, who is said to have worn so many jewels that she sparkled from a distance, had her own emerald mines.

Of the more than four thousand minerals in the world, relatively few are used as gems. To qualify, the stone needs to be rare, have good clarity (meaning it has no or few defects), and be tough enough to resist scratching. A gem must be durable as well as beautiful.

A gem's value is determined by the four Cs: clarity, cut, color, and carat. The clearer the gem, the more valuable. The cut is important because it helps bring out the gem's sparkle and color. For many diamonds, the preferred color is clear—though they can reflect myriads of color as light passes through them. **Gemologists** assign grades to color using strict standards and lighting.

IT'S A CARAT NOT A CARROT

Gemstones are measured in units called carats—not the carrots you eat. One carat weighs 0.2 grams, a fraction of an ounce. Now if only your carrots came in that small of a serving!

YELLOW CRYSTALLINE CALCITE

WHAT MAKES A MINERAL A GEM?

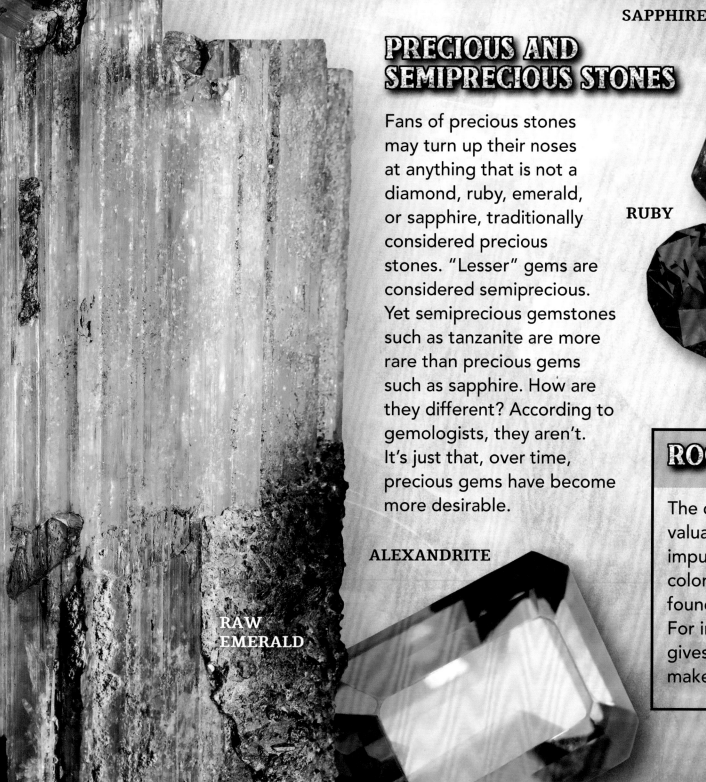

SAPPHIRE

PRECIOUS AND SEMIPRECIOUS STONES

Fans of precious stones may turn up their noses at anything that is not a diamond, ruby, emerald, or sapphire, traditionally considered precious stones. "Lesser" gems are considered semiprecious. Yet semiprecious gemstones such as tanzanite are more rare than precious gems such as sapphire. How are they different? According to gemologists, they aren't. It's just that, over time, precious gems have become more desirable.

RUBY

TANZANITE

ALEXANDRITE

RAW EMERALD

ROCK-HARD FACT

The clearer a gem, the more valuable, right? But it's actually impurities that give gems their colors. Impurities are **elements** found in small amounts in gems. For instance, the chromium that gives rubies their red hue can make alexandrite appear purple.

5

Gems are so rare because they require a very specific set of ideal circumstances—time, pressure, space, and temperature—for their creation. Most gemstones form in Earth's exterior layer or crust, which is no more than 25 mi. (40 km) thick. Only two gemstones, diamond and peridot, form in Earth's **mantle**.

As **magma** cools beneath the surface, it can crystallize, resulting in minerals. With the right amount of time and pressure, gems such as quartz, beryl, garnet, and topaz can result.

Magma comes to the surface as lava, an **igneous** rock, and becomes subject to erosion or pressure as it gets buried under sediment. Gems produced from **sedimentary** rock include opals and zircon.

Pressure within the earth can change the crystal structure in igneous and sedimentary minerals, resulting in **metamorphic** rocks. The results—gemstones such as rubies, sapphires, and turquoise—can be stunning.

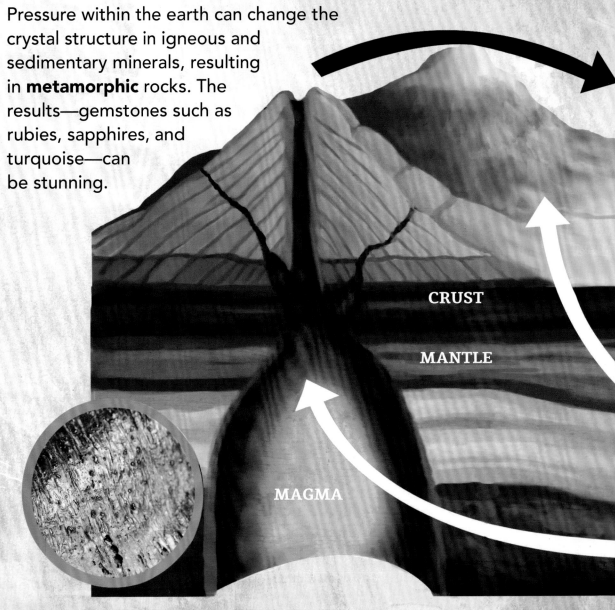

CRUST

MANTLE

MAGMA

IGNEOUS

BEAUTY UNDER PRESSURE

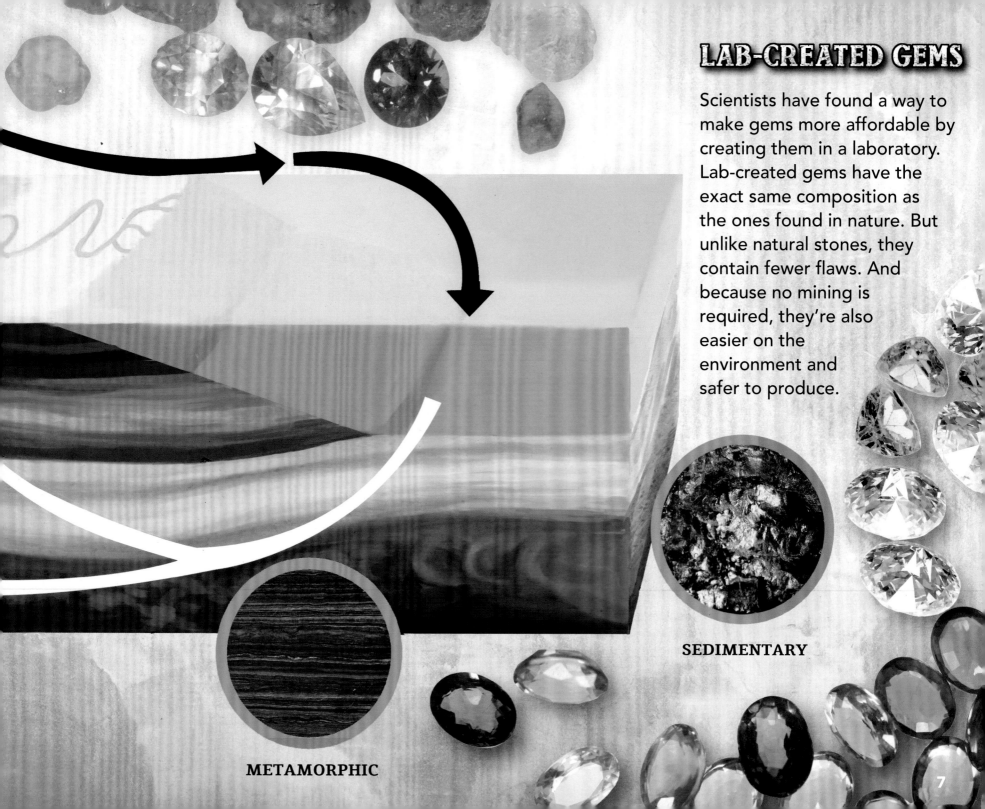

LAB-CREATED GEMS

Scientists have found a way to make gems more affordable by creating them in a laboratory. Lab-created gems have the exact same composition as the ones found in nature. But unlike natural stones, they contain fewer flaws. And because no mining is required, they're also easier on the environment and safer to produce.

SEDIMENTARY

METAMORPHIC

On the Mohs scale of mineral hardness, gems rank highest of all minerals. Diamonds, made of pure carbon, rank the highest of all gems. They are so hard that they can cut just about everything. But hardness isn't the only way to classify minerals.

ROCK-HARD FACT

Diamonds have long been known as the world's hardest material. But they may have a little competition. Wurtzite boron nitride and lonsdaleite minerals with similar compositions to diamonds are much harder. However, so little of either substance can be found or has been made in labs that diamonds are still the favorite—for now.

SIX PROPERTIES OF MINERALS

1. Specific gravity: How heavy is it compared with the same amount of water?

2. Luster: Is it shiny . . . or dull?

3. Transparency: Can you shine a flashlight through it?

4. Hardness: How hard is it? Can you scratch it with your fingernail or could it scratch you—or even glass? Check out our hardness scale on page 9.

5. Color: What color is it? Some minerals, such as beryl, come in different colors.

EMERALD BERYL

AQUAMARINE BERYL

6. Streak: When you rub it across a rough surface, what color streak does it make? The streak test shows the mineral's true color.

HOW TO MEASURE MINERAL

PUT YOUR GEMS TO THE TEST

Do a streak test. Do you want to know what color your gems really are? Rub your rock across the unglazed side of a white bathroom or kitchen tile or the bottom of a white ceramic coffee mug. What color is the streak? Your gem's streak color is considered its true color.

Do a scratch test. Let's see how hard your gems are. Try scratching one gem with another one. Which one left a mark? Your answer will reveal the hardest of the two. Try scratching the harder gem on your third sample. The one that leaves a scratch mark on the other two is the hardest gem—and possibly the most valuable!

MOHS SCALE OF MINERAL HARDNESS

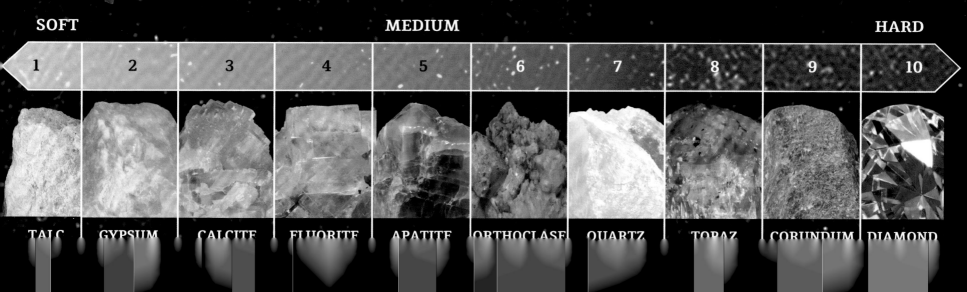

SOFT				MEDIUM					HARD
1	2	3	4	5	6	7	8	9	10
TALC	GYPSUM	CALCITE	FLUORITE	APATITE	ORTHOCLASE	QUARTZ	TOPAZ	CORUNDUM	DIAMOND

Unlike rocks and minerals, gems are elusive. Though many are found beneath the earth in mines where few of us dare go, some find their way to the surface and are exposed by weathering and erosion. Some become exposed as the result of the construction of high-rises, tunnels, and railroads.

Mountainous regions of New York, Montana, North Carolina, and Nevada are frequent haunts of gem enthusiasts, as is the volcanic ground of Crater of Diamonds State Park in Arkansas. In 2011 alone, more than five hundred diamonds were found at the park, where visitors are able to keep what they find. In October 2016, a father and daughter found a 2-carat diamond after being at the park for less than an hour.

Gems, in fact, are plentiful in areas prone to earthquakes and **volcanoes**, where many are formed. They also can be found fairly readily in a region of Australia, where rough sapphires lie just below the topsoil—no digging required!

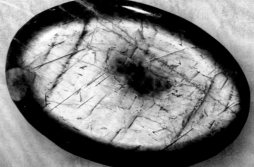

LABRADORITE

ROUGH AND READY

AQUAMARINE

TOPAZ

TOURMALINE

BY THE BOOK

Rough gems look very different from their cut-and-polished counterparts. Sometimes they're even hidden within rocks. A pocket guidebook can help you distinguish a gemstone from a regular mineral.

RUBY

When it comes to gemstones, a hefty size draws a hefty price. At 840 lbs. (381 kg), or a whopping 1.9 million carats, the Bahia emerald is the largest gemstone ever found. The stone, which weighs about as much as a cow, is worth $400 million—way more than the price of a cow!

The title of the largest **faceted** diamond ever found belongs to the Golden Jubilee Diamond. Though it doesn't compare in size with the hefty Bahia emerald, it still measures 545.67 carats—especially impressive compared with 1-carat gems commonly found in jewelry. It is valued between $4 million and $12 million.

A giant ball of glow-in-the-dark fluorite known as "the pearl" ranks as the largest semiprecious stone ever found. Weighing 6 tons (5.4 tonnes) and measuring 5 ft. 3 in. (1.6 m) in diameter, the green orb is worth $301 million and required three years of grinding to achieve its shape.

THE PEARL

GOLDEN JUBILEE DIAMOND

BAHIA EMERALD

SOME FOR THE RECORD

THE TOP TEN MOST EXPENSIVE DIAMONDS IN THE WORLD

1. **The Koh-I-Noor Diamond**, clear diamond, 105 carats, price: PRICELESS

2. **The Sancy Diamond**, pale yellow diamond, 55.23 carats, price: PRICELESS

3. **The Cullinan Diamond**, clear diamond, 3,106.75 carats, price: $400 million

4. **The Hope Diamond**, blue diamond, 45.52 carats, price: $350 million

5. **The De Beers Centenary Diamond**, clear diamond, 273.85 carats, price: $100 million

6. **The Regent Diamond**, white with pale blue diamond, 140.64 carats, price: $60.2 million

7. **The Oppenheimer Blue Diamond**, blue diamond, 14.62 carats, price: $57.5 million

8. **The Steinmetz Pink Diamond**, vivid pink diamond, 59.6 carats, price: $25 million

9. **The Taylor-Burton Diamond**, white diamond, 68 carats, price: $18.9 million

10. **The Wittelsbach Diamond**, blue diamond, 35.36 carats, price: $16.4 million

THE HOPE DIAMOND

Stories of beheadings, murders, and accidents of its many owners surround the mysterious, deep-blue Hope Diamond. At 45.52 carats, its history and unusual color make the value of the so-called cursed stone hard to determine. Also hard to determine is the truth of the legend surrounding it. Were the stories made up to increase the diamond's value?

ROCK-HARD FACT

Since 1958, the Hope Diamond has been on display at the Smithsonian National Museum of Natural History in Washington, DC with no effects of a curse on its caretakers.

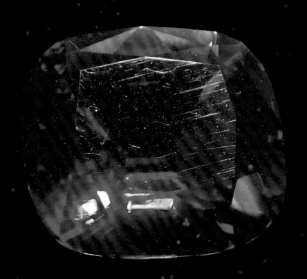

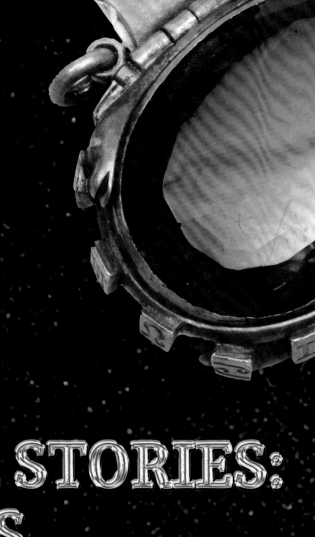

STRANGE-BUT-TRUE STORIES: DEADLY GEMSTONES

THE DELHI PURPLE SAPPHIRE

Nineteenth-century author Edward Heron-Allen refused to believe in curses until he became the owner of the Delhi Purple Sapphire, a gem he decided was "stained with blood." Heron-Allen, claiming the gem had caused him to be "trebly accursed," gave away the stone twice, only to have it returned to him because of the bad luck it brought the new owners. He then threw it into a canal, only to have it found and returned to him three months later. Finally he sealed the cursed jewel in a box and donated it to a museum with strict instructions that it not be opened until three years after his death—and that his daughter never touch it.

THE KOH-I-NOOR DIAMOND

Much blood has been shed to win the right to this 105.6-carat diamond, now set in a British crown. According to Hindu legend, "He who owns this diamond will own the world, but will also know all its misfortunes. Only God or woman can wear it with impunity." The jewel has long been worn only by women—just to be safe.

Raw gemstones may cost thousands of dollars a carat but still may only look like colorful rocks to the untrained eye. They require careful cutting and polishing in a process called **lapidary**. The work is slow but also hard—hard because such stones are often as tough as steel.

The gem cutter must choose the cut that will bring out the jewel's **brilliance**. He also must consider the crystal shape of the gem, as well as any defects found within it. He then cuts it in a way that enhances its color and beauty while best preserving its size.

ROCK-HARD FACT

Most gemstones lose between 55 and 75 percent of their original weight when cut. A 5-carat rough gemstone can be reduced to a 1-carat cut-and-polished jewel.

NO GETTING 'ROUND IT

The crystal shapes of rubies usually make it impossible to use a brilliant (or cone-shaped) cut on them without losing too much weight, which also means a loss in value. That's why rubies are typically cut into ovals.

THE PERFECT CUT

PEAR CUT

PUTTING THEIR BEST FACETS FORWARD

BRILLIANT
CUT

RADIANT CUT

MARQUISE
CUT

BAGUETTE
CUT

HEART CUT

CABOCHON

OVAL CUT

PRINCESS CUT

HIGH DOME
CABOCHON

You may not have the tools or experience you need for lapidary, but you still can bring out the shine of your gemstones using things you have around your house.

WHAT YOU NEED

- Bowl of warm water
- Soft cloth
- Soft brush, such as an old toothbrush

WHAT TO DO

1. Soak the gemstone in warm water for an hour.
2. Using the soft cloth, gently dry the stone.
3. Dip the toothbrush in the water, and very gently brush the gemstone to clean crevices.
4. Let the gem air-dry.

POLISHING YOUR GEMS

TAKE A CLOSER LOOK

Now that your gemstones are shiny, try looking at them from different angles under different types of light—next to a window facing the sun in the daytime, under a lamp in the daytime, under a lamp in a dark room, outside in natural light at different times of day, or under an ultraviolet light if you have one. With an adult's help, you could even compare the colors by candlelight. How do the colors change in different types of light?

HERE'S A TIP!

Use a magnifying glass, if available, to study the changing colors within your stone—but only use it indoors! A magnifying glass will make heat from the sunlight so intense it could crack your gemstone. Compare the colors you see using a magnifying glass with those you see using your naked eye.

Gems get their color based on how much light they absorb. The more light that passes through a gem, the lighter its color. A diamond, for instance, will appear clear and without color when all the colors of light pass through it. Darker gems absorb more light.

CHROMIUM

RUBY

EMERALD

DIAMOND

Rubies absorb all light except red, so they appear red. Likewise, emeralds appear green because they absorb everything but green light. But what causes these gems to absorb the colors they do? It's the metal chromium. Different amounts of the metal produce different colors in each of the gems.

COLOR THEM AMAZING

GARNET

SAPPHIRE

PERIDOT

Metals give many gems their special colors. Different amounts of the metal iron give sapphires, garnets, and peridots their blue, deep red, and green hues. Sapphires are made even more beautiful with the addition of a little titanium.

IRON

TITANIUM

TURQUOISE

COPPER

Turquoise, considered a semiprecious gem, gets its trademark blue-green color from the copper within it.

For centuries, gemstones—once too precious for common people to own—became the objects of lore and legends. They were sought not only for their beauty but also for their mysterious powers.

AMBER

Amber was once the favorite of magicians who wanted greater powers. It also was believed to make people calmer, happier, and stronger.

JADE

Long life, friendship, protection while traveling, luck, and wisdom are a few of the benefits people once hoped to gain by wearing jade. The green semiprecious stone has long been a favorite in China, where it is used in carvings as well as jewelry.

STRANGE-BUT-TRUE STORIES: LORE AND LEGENDS

BERYL

Beryl, which comes in many colors, was once believed to keep people happy, healthy, young-looking, hard-working, and safe from evil spirits.

EMERALD

If someone wanted to be smarter, have better memory, or be able to predict the future, emeralds were the stone of choice. The green jewel was also said to cure eye diseases and protect children from certain ailments.

TOPAZ

The ancient Greeks believed a topaz made you invisible—a helpful skill in battle—while the ancient Romans believed it improved eyesight. During the Middle Ages, people actually believed the stone could prevent death.

AMETHYST

The amethyst was long thought to promote mental health, cure headaches, provide good hearing, and ensure good sleep. It even was said to help you have good dreams while you're getting all that good sleep.

The beauty, color, and sparkle of gems make it no wonder they have inspired centuries of lore and legend—not to mention conflict and coveting. From clear to black with every imaginable color in between, gems represent some of the most remarkable, versatile, and durable products of nature.

TURQUOISE

AMMOLITE

JASPER

YELLOW TOURMALINE

SMOKY QUARTZ

MOONSTONE

SUGILITE

AMAZONITE

A GALLERY OF GEMS

CHAROITE

METEORITE

ZIRCON

TANZANITE

HEMATITE

CITRINE

WHAT IS YOUR BIRTHSTONE?

JANUARY
GARNET

FEBRUARY
AMETHYST

MARCH
AQUAMARINE

APRIL
DIAMOND

MAY
EMERALD

JUNE
PEARL

JULY
RUBY

AUGUST
PERIDOT

SEPTEMBER
SAPPHIRE

OCTOBER
TOURMALINE

NOVEMBER
CITRINE

DECEMBER
BLUE TOPAZ

Birthstones are gemstones that are associated with months of birth. Can you spot your birthstone?

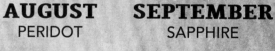

Just as Hollywood has its stars, so does the gem world. Some of these have belonged to royalty, but each has achieved a level of royalty all its own.

CARTIER HALO TIARA

One of many bejeweled tiaras belonging to the British royal family, this diamond-studded piece was an eighteenth birthday gift to Queen Elizabeth. Kate Middleton wore it when she married Prince William.

HEART OF THE OCEAN

Made for the 1997 movie *Titanic,* the design of this blue diamond necklace was inspired by the infamous Hope Diamond. (See page 14.) The original necklace contains a 15-carat diamond and is worth about $20 million, but several replicas were made using 170-carat sapphires as the center stone.

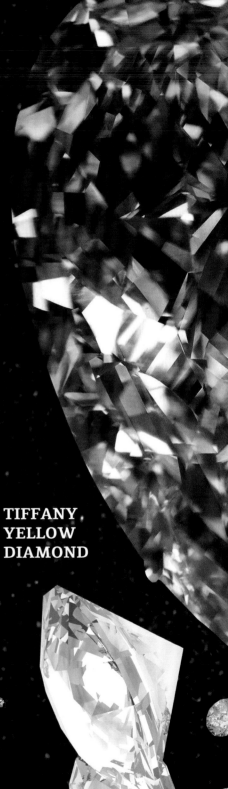

TIFFANY YELLOW DIAMOND

STARS OF THE SHOW

PANTHER BRACELET

Known as the world's most expensive bracelet, this realistic design is filled with diamonds and onyx. The eyes are made of emeralds. Once belonging to King Edward III of England, the bracelet sold for $6.2 million at auction.

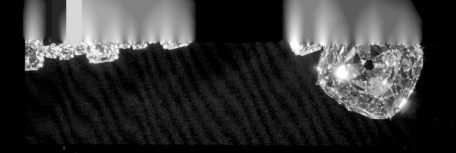

TIFFANY YELLOW

Believed to have been worn only twice, this 128-carat jewel ranks as the world's second-largest yellow diamond. Set in a necklace, it is on display at Tiffany & Co. **jeweler** in New York City and has been valued at $12 million.

QUEEN MARY'S DIAMOND RIVIERE

Translated as "river of diamonds," this $1.8 million necklace that once belonged to the British royal family contains thirty-four diamonds set in gold and silver.

PRINCESS DIANA'S RING

This 18-carat sapphire surrounded by seventeen round diamonds became famous with the engagement of Great Britain's Prince Charles and Princess Diana in 1981. Their son, Prince William, has since given the ring to his bride, Kate Middleton, in

When most people think of diamonds, they think of clear, glimmering, glass-like stones. These colorless stones have captured the hearts and imagination of people for centuries.

But it is not color, or lack of color, that makes a diamond what it is. It's the gem's makeup. Diamonds are formed deep within earth's mantle from pure carbon atoms that are arranged in a way that makes the gems incredibly hard. **Geologists** believe eruptions of volcanoes then push diamonds closer to the surface.

Diamonds also come in a variety of shades of yellow, with the Tiffany Yellow (see pages 26–27) being at the brightest end of the spectrum.

Brown diamonds, sometimes known as chocolate diamonds, have recently grown in popularity.

A CLOSER LOOK: DIAMONDS

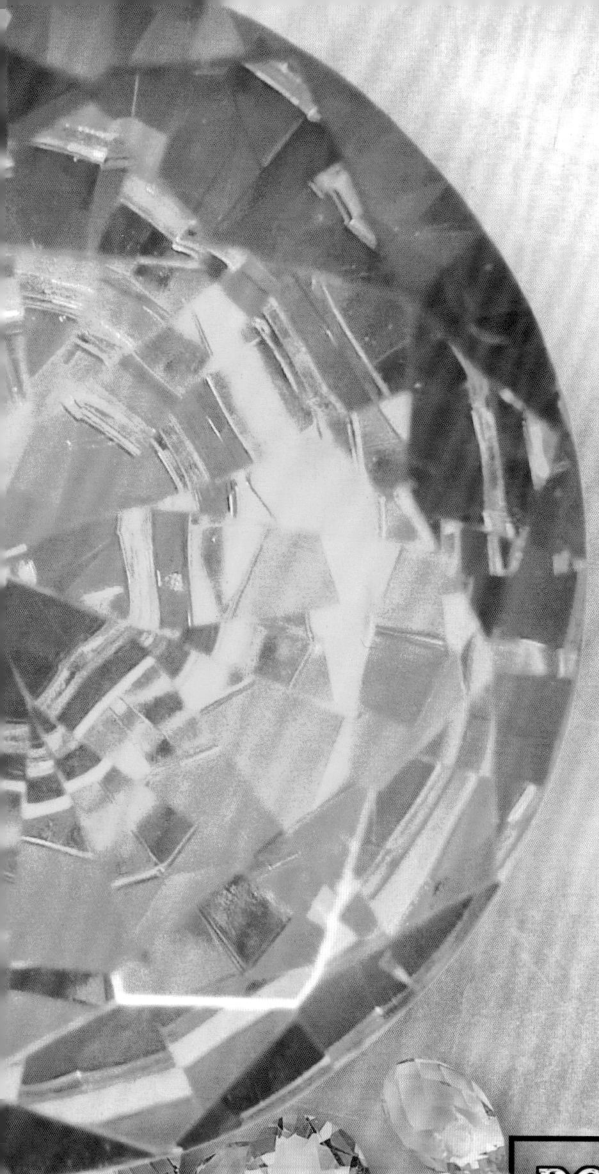

In addition to clear, yellow, and brown, diamonds come in every color of the rainbow.

PINK

RED

ORANGE

GREEN

BLUE

VIOLET

GRAY

Some diamonds are actually a combination of colors. In fact, with twelve base colors of diamonds, there are an estimated 7,380 colors of diamonds!

FANCY BLACK

CLEAR

ROCK-HARD FACT

The 14.62-carat Oppenheimer Blue diamond, a vivid blue diamond described as one of the rarest in the world, set a world record in May 2016 as the most expensive jewel ever sold at auction. Its price: a whopping $57.5 million!

When we see someone with deep blue eyes, we might describe their eyes as sapphire blue. That's because deep blue is the most common color of sapphires, a gem beloved by royalty for centuries. The more vivid the color, the more valued the sapphire.

PINK

ORANGE

PURPLE

YELLOW

GREEN

But like diamonds, sapphires actually come in a variety of colors. Fancy-colored sapphires, as they're called, come in green, orange, yellow, pink, purple, and many colors in between—almost every color except red. That's because sapphires belong to the family of the mineral corundum. A red gem made of corundum is always a ruby, a cousin to the sapphire.

A CLOSER LOOK: SAPPHIRES

One of the most valuable sapphires of all isn't the well-known deep-blue color. It's a pink-orange color known as a *padparadscha*, a word that means "lotus blossom" in Sinhalese. The language is spoken by people who live in Sri Lanka, where many of these rare stones are found.

ROCK-HARD FACT

Measuring 9 on the Mohs scale of mineral hardness, sapphires are so durable that they were used in windows on a Pioneer Venus spacecraft launched in 1978.

Sapphires are found in parts of Asia, Africa, and Australia. They are also found throughout the state of Montana, where they were discovered during the Gold Rushes of the 1860s. People searching to make their fortunes with gold would toss aside what they called "nuisance pebbles" until 1865, when an **appraiser** with Tiffany & Co. identified them as sapphires. He described the jewels as "the finest precious gemstones ever found in the United States." Miners then found themselves making more money in sapphires than in gold.

Second in hardness to a diamond, rubies can cost more than a diamond of the same size because of their rarity. These members of the mineral corundum family vary in color from pinkish to nearly purple, but the trademark deep-red color—known as pigeon's blood—is the most valuable.

In May 2015, a 25.59-carat pigeon's blood ruby described as "among the rarest of gems" sold for $30.3 million at auction, setting a new record as the world's most valuable ruby.

The Sanskrit word for ruby, *ratnaraj*, means "king of gems." Rubies have long been treasured by royalty. This crown once belonged to Marie Alexandrovna, a former duchess and daughter of a Russian tsar.

It's not just the rarity and color of rubies that makes them special. They're **fluorescent** under ultraviolet light, making their color appear more intense in daylight.

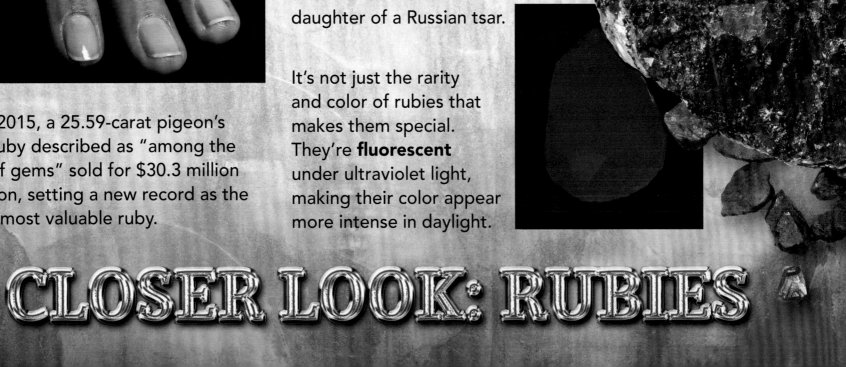

A CLOSER LOOK: RUBIES

Some of the most valuable rubies in the world remain in their rough states. Said to be one of the world's most perfect ruby crystals, the 196.10-carat Hixon Ruby Crystal is on display at the Natural History Museum of Los Angeles. The slightly smaller 167-carat Edwardes Ruby, once owned by an art critic, is now on display at the Natural History Museum of London.

HIXON RUBY CRYSTAL **EDWARDES RUBY**

In honor of the fiftieth anniversary of *The Wizard of Oz*, jeweler Harry Winston created slippers like the ones worn by actress Judy Garland that are made of real rubies—4,600 of them. With a total weight of 1,350 carats in rubies plus 50 carats of diamond accents, the shoes are valued at $3 million.

ROCK-HARD FACT

In some parts of Asia and Africa, rubies and diamonds are mined and sold to fund conflicts that hurt and even kill innocent people. Some children and adults are forced to mine the gems to raise money for armies. Gems mined in this manner are known as blood rubies or blood diamonds.

People throughout history from Cleopatra to actress Elizabeth Taylor have been enchanted by emeralds. The lower **density** of emeralds gives buyers more to love: A 1-carat emerald will be slightly larger than a 1-carat diamond.

These bright green stones are often fashioned in rectangular cuts because of their crystal shape. They are known for their flaws. Though they rank 7.5 to 8 on the Mohs scale of mineral hardness, they are also very brittle and can crack if not treated with great care.

Emeralds are chromium-rich examples of the mineral beryl. Their green color sets them apart from other beryls. But how much green does a beryl need to be considered an emerald? Gem experts can't agree, but the preferred color range is bluish green to pure, vivid green. Anything lighter than that is called a green beryl.

A CLOSER LOOK: EMERALDS

Many emeralds, like the famous Patricia Emerald, are found in Colombia in South America. This raw twelve-sided gemstone, weighing 632 carats, is on display at the American Museum of Natural History in New York City.

PATRICIA EMERALD

ROCK-HARD FACT

In 1985, diver Mel Fisher found treasure from Spanish ships *Nuestra Senora de Atocha* and *Santa Margarita*, which sank in a hurricane off the Florida coast in 1622. The sunken ships left behind millions upon millions of dollars in gold and jewels, including this emerald cross and emerald ring.

DIAMONDS

Only about three of every ten diamonds found is gem quality. Most diamonds are too flawed, oddly shaped, small, or poorly colored to be used as jewels. But the hardness of diamonds ensures none will go to waste.

Because they can cut through almost anything, industrial-grade diamonds are used in drill bits and saw blades. The structure of diamonds also helps improve sound quality in speakers. Since diamonds are heat- and abrasion-resistant, they are used to make windows for X-ray machines, lasers, and vacuum chambers. They are also useful in electronics as well as in polishing and grinding.

STRANGE-BUT-TRUE STORIES: BEAUTIFUL AND USEFUL GEMS

Amethyst, tiger's eye, and citrine are all members of the quartz family and are also valued gemstones. But the prettier members of the quartz family have no reason to look down at their plainer cousins. Not-so-ordinary quartz has a multitude of industrial uses, ranging from making glass to mining natural gas. Measuring 7 on the Mohs scale of mineral hardness, quartz can be used as an abrasive or even as sand.

But one of the most interesting ways quartz is used is in clocks, watches, and electronics. Quartz clocks and watches are more accurate than other timepieces, and quartz crystals can be found in cellphones, computers, games, and other electronics. Chances are good you can find this useful mineral in your own home.

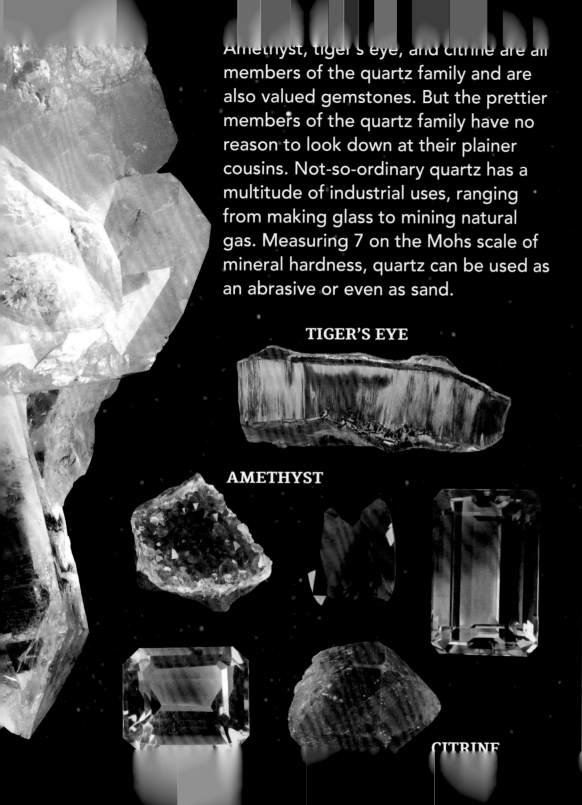

TIGER'S EYE

AMETHYST

CITRINE

ROCK-HARD FACT

In 1969, a ruby-powered laser beam one hundred thousand times as bright as the sun was successfully bounced off the moon. The laser helped scientists understand more about the moon and will help them understand more about other moons and planets. Modern lasers use different minerals to produce different types of laser beams.

Gems, as a rule, are inorganic. But some gems break that rule. Pearls, for instance, are made by living animals. When an irritant gets inside the shell of a **mollusk**, such as an oyster, the animal coats it with the lining of its shell, known as mother-of-pearl. The pearl grows bigger as more layers are added.

ROCK-HARD FACT

Some cultures have long believed bamboo coral has healing properties—and maybe for good reason. Scientists are studying ways to use bamboo coral in repairing human bones, and they are also trying to find ways to use their coral skeletons in medicine.

In 2016, a Filipino man remembered a 75 lb. (34 kg) pearl he had hidden under his bed. The pearl had been set aside for ten years, until the man was preparing to move. The giant gem, which measures 2.2 ft. (67 cm) long and is 1 ft. (30 cm) wide, may be the world's largest pearl.

A CLOSER LOOK: PEARLS, CORAL, AND AMBER

Found in shades of red, white, black, or blue, coral is formed from the hardened skeletons of coral **organisms** known as polyps. These creatures live in limestone reefs they build in warm tropical waters. But the harvesting of coral for jewelry is reducing the number of reefs, which act as **habitats** for many sea creatures and plant life. Some people have created coral farms to meet the need of the jewelry industry.

Amber is ancient fossilized tree sap, often found preserved in a type of sedimentary rock called shale or washed up on a beach. Occurring in colors ranging from brown to yellow to red, amber is soft enough to be easily scratched, yet it has been treasured throughout history. Roman gladiators believed amber would give them success in battle.

Because of the way it forms, amber can become a time capsule for ancient air and water, as well as living things such as lizards and insects. In the fictional movie *Jurassic Park*, scientists recreated dinosaurs by using DNA they had extracted from amber.

Quartz, the product of the elements oxygen and silicon, is the most common mineral on the planet— and also one of the most useful. (See page 37.)

Naturally colorless, quartz becomes beautiful with the help of impurities that result in colorful gemstones.

Getting its name from the citron fruit, citrine—not to be confused with the topaz—is known for its yellow and orange colors. As with amethyst, the deeper the color, the more valuable the stone.

TOPAZ   **CITRINE**

Amethysts are the most valued of all quartz gemstones. The deeper the purple, the more valuable the jewel. Considered a royal jewel by ancient Egyptians, amethysts were believed to increase power and were used in Cleopatra's seal.

AMETHYST

A CLOSER LOOK: QUARTZ

Thin bands of minerals within this quartz gemstone give it its distinctive cat's eye effect—the bright, narrow slit similar to what you would observe in your pet cat. Gemologists call this effect chatoyance based on the French word *chatoyer* (CHA-toy-ay), which means "to shine like a cat's eye."

CAT'S EYE

ROCK-HARD FACT

Quartz makes up about 12 percent of Earth's crust. About 70 percent of all sand is made from quartz that has been worn by erosion.

TIGER'S EYE

RUTILATED QUARTZ

JASPER

When most people think of garnets, they think of a blood-red gemstone that is similar to—but less expensive than—the ruby. Its name even comes from an old Latin word that means "dark red." But garnets actually include a whole group of gemstones in a variety of colors and hardnesses.

It's the minerals within the garnets that make the difference. Garnets that contain calcium or uvarovite are usually softer and green in color. Replace the calcium or uvarovite with iron, manganese, or aluminum, and you'll have a harder stone that is likely to be red. Other minerals result in brown, purple, pink, yellow, orange, black, and even rare clear gemstones. An especially rare blue garnet was found in Madagascar, where many garnets are mined.

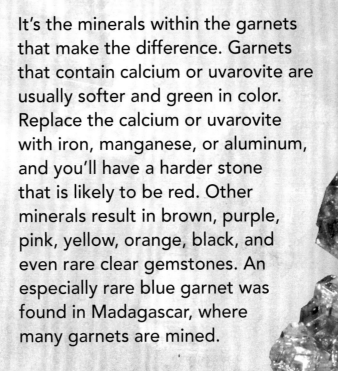

A CLOSER LOOK: GARNET

Garnets were once among the most widely traded gems. In the Middle Ages, they found favor among the wealthy and powerful. In ancient Rome, important documents were sealed using garnet rings dipped in wax.

ROCK-HARD FACT

If you can't decide what your favorite garnet is, just choose a color-changing stone. A hybrid of minerals causes this rare and valuable garnet to shift color dramatically depending upon the lighting.

In the desert region of Australia known as the Outback, seasonal rains soak deep into the ground, leaving deposits of silica. As the ground dries, the silica deposits form into opals. Almost all of the world's opals come from Australia.

The silica within the opals creates an unusual effect known as play-of-color that causes light to reflect a flashing rainbow. The color depends upon the size of tiny spheres within the stone. Smaller spheres produce a violet hue and larger ones produce red, with the remaining colors of the rainbow

THE AUSTRALIAN OUTBACK

displayed among the various sizes in between. Because opals can contain the colors of all other gems, Romans considered them the most precious of all gemstones.

A CLOSER LOOK: OPALS

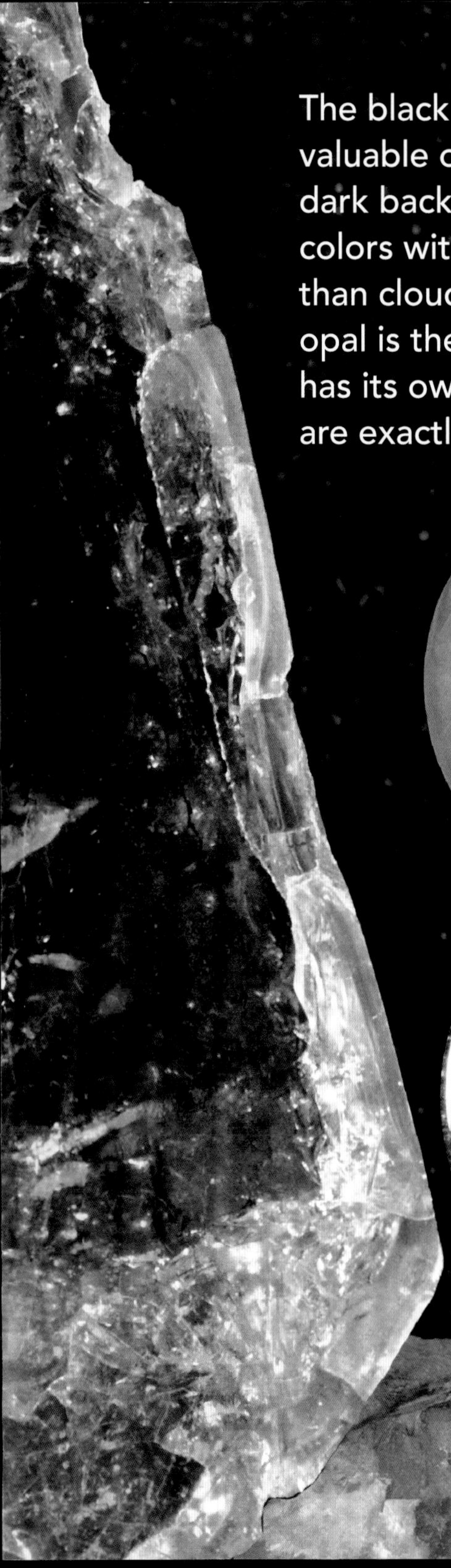

The black opal is among the most valuable of all because of the way the dark background brings out the dancing colors within. Clear opals are more valued than cloudy ones, and the common white opal is the most affordable. Each variety has its own qualities, and no two opals are exactly alike.

CLEAR OPAL

BLACK OPAL

ROCK-HARD FACT

Because opals form as the result of heavy rains, part of their early beginnings remain forever within them. About one-fifth of their weight is in water.

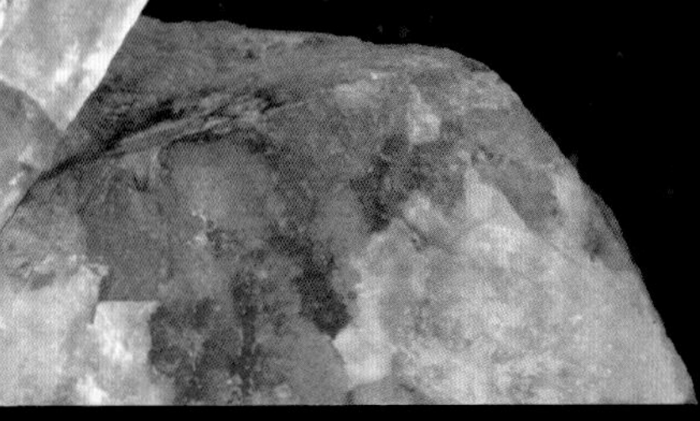

APPRAISER
someone who determines the value or quality of something such as gems

ATOM
the smallest unit of matter

BRILLIANCE
ability to reflect light to bring out color

DENSITY
the amount of mass in a certain space

ELEMENT
a substance found in nature that is in its simplest form

EROSION
the process in which wind, water, and ice wear away rock over time

FACET
flat-cut surface

FLUORESCENT
appearing to glow

GEMOLOGIST
someone who studies precious stones

GEOLOGIST
an expert in the study of Earth's makeup and physical history

HABITAT
an animal's natural home or environment

IGNEOUS
rock formed from cooled magma or lava

INORGANIC
not coming from living things

JEWELER
a person or company that makes or sells jewels or jewelry

GLOSSARY

LAPIDARY
the process of cutting and polishing gemstones

MAGMA
hot liquid found beneath Earth's crust

MANTLE
the hot rock between Earth's crust and core that makes up 83 percent of Earth's volume

METAMORPHIC
rock formed by heat and pressure from sedimentary and igneous rock

MINERAL
a hard material from which rocks and gems are made that is found in nature and is not made of living things

MOLLUSK
a class of animals that includes oysters, mussels, snails, slugs and octupuses

ORGANISM
a life form, whether a plant, animal, or single-celled creature

SEDIMENTARY
made from sediment deposited by wind or water

UNIFORM
the same throughout

VOLCANO
a mountain or hill from which hot gas or vapor, rocks, and lava erupt from deep within the earth

Written by C.J. McDonald
Designed by Brie Nagy
Cover Design by Ali Castro

tangerine Press

SCHOLASTIC

Copyright © 2017 Scholastic Inc.

Scholastic, Tangerine Press, and associated logos are trademarks and/or registered trademarks of Scholastic Inc.

Published by Tangerine Press, an imprint of Scholastic Inc.
557 Broadway
New York, NY 10012

10 9 8 7 6 5 4 3

ISBN: 978-1-338-16625-5

Printed in Guangzhou, China